The Immaculate Perception

THE
IMMACULATE
PERCEPTION

Christopher Dewdney

For Sharon,

love

Christopher

Anansi

Toronto   Buffalo   London   Sydney

Author photograph: Paul Orenstein
Cover design: Laurel Angeloff
Cover and text illustrations: Christopher Dewdney

Published with assistance from the Canada Council and the Ontario Arts Council, and printed in Canada for

> House of Anansi Press Limited
> 35 Britain Street
> Toronto, Ontario M5A 1R7

Canadian Cataloguing in Publication Data

Dewdney, Christopher, 1951-
  The immaculate perception
ISBN 0-88784-151-1
I. Title.
PS8557.E846I65 1986   C814'.54   C86-094683-5
PR9199.3.D48I65 1986

1 2 3 4 5   96 95 94 93 92 91 90   89 88 87 86

The whole organism can be considered as a coded representation of its environment. We can say that the wings of a bird 'represent' the air and the legs of man the land, and similarly that their brains contain representations in code that allow them to fly or walk, and their nerves carry code messages about relevant features of the world.

— J.Z. Young

Contents

Foreword

These bits, aphorisms, essays and verbal 'takes' are constellated around a larger theme, which is, roughly, the spectacle of consciousness embracing its own materiality. It also deals with the reverse notion, consciousness being duplicated by technology, matter mimicking mind.

Science is holding up an increasingly clearer mirror to ourselves and like vampires our reflections are gradually fading into pure difference, invisible against the background of total phenomenology.

> The housefly is a miracle of miniaturization.
> Nature is the divine technology.

Human Consciousness

Consciousness is an illusion generated by the highest integrative function of our nervous system, the mind.

The sense of self, human consciousness, is like a virtual image: it exists solely by relation to an observer. Its singular disposition is determined by the observer hypothetically observing himself or herself in the act of self-observation. This is the double enclosure of self-consciousness.

Self-observation can exist only ideally, as a kind of privileged shadow-boxing. Existence in any mode other than the virtual would expose the inherent paradox on which the whole show is based. The proposed universality of this utterly private experience is qualified by a presumed congruence among observers who are members of the same species. Language is the armature of this congruence.

Consciousness is a set of footprints in the snow which stop & then retrace themselves.

Mind as Standing Wave

The millions of neurons which make up the cortex of both hemispheres have a tendency to synchronize their discharges in electric ripples of excitation. These synchronized trains of neuronal pulses are known as brain waves and have three major modes based on their frequencies. The slowest is the *theta* rhythm which is associated with the functioning of the thalamus in the upper brain stem, a junction of sorts for the activity of the brain. Its frequency is in the range of 5 to 6 cycles per second. The next level is the *delta* rhythm which is associated with sleep. At the third level are *alpha* waves, which have a frequency of 8 to 13 cycles per second and are typical of the electrical activity in the brain of a mature, conscious human. Consciousness is characterized by a long persisting phase constancy of alpha waves. This vast co-ordination of neurons is similar to metachronal waves in millipedes, where the synchronizing of hundreds of legs is processed in waveform.

Knots

The brain is constructed out of the very reality it perceives. It must then, perforce, be a recursive structure, a knotting of that reality, such that somehow, through some form of topological twisting of space, matter attains the property of self-observation. This is like making something out of nothing.

The Immaculate Perception

Consciousness requires the immaculate 'separateness' of objects of its attention. It is necessary that the boundaries of the 'object' are clear, in order to fortify its identity, its distinction from the matrix.

Identity is signification.

Perception, the actual neurochemical process of the nervous system, is not as specific as the *ideal* of signified attention ascribed to as 'consciousness'. There comes a point, a tactile limen, when you can't distinguish between two fingers and one as they are pressed into your back. This demonstrates a lower-level discrimination limit, an equipment limitation, where the sensory system can't resolve fine detail.

The specificity of consciousness, the 'I' perceived, is also diffuse. It is generated by the same neurochemical process as perception. Specificity in vision, for instance, is a result of the resolution of a mosaic signal within the visual cortex. The mosaic signal is characteristic of the entire nervous system. Its granular nature in vision is revealed by aberrant states, such as 'mosaic vision' in migraines and 'pointillistic vision' as induced by both migraines and hallucinogenic drugs. The diffuse specificity of both consciousness & perception sensuously irritates signified or ideal consciousness.

Another aspect of this sensuous irritation is revealed by certain pathological obsessions induced by two neurotransmitter mimetic drugs, d-lysergic acid diethylamide and methamphetamine. This obsessive behaviour, called *punding,* such as picking hairs out of a rug, cobwebs out of hair, sand out of sugar, dead skin from live or sorting trivial objects according to class, is animated by consciousness in a reinforcement of 'ideal' signified attention running upstream against the 'flow' of the mosaic signal.

Punding and hypervigilance, consequences of generalized C.N.S. excitation, are echoed on a larger scale by the 'sorting' preoccupation. This is a tendency of all human groups to isolate independently occurring elements of nature, such as corn or boars, and gather them together in species multiples over and above the quantities necessary for survival. In this act, a function of hypervigilance, we have the origin of both mathematics and science.

Signified consciousness, fervent with the immanence of ideation and signification, worries away at the fuzziness of the mysterious boundaries of identity.

simultaneous   multiple   indivisible

Form

Form, being intrinsically sub-divisible—*i.e.,* perpetually at the interface of matter and energy—exists only as a perceptual generalization.

The Object

Because of equipment limitations, perception is confined to a selective sample of a more extensive continuum. Noetically, an object can only be as specific as the sum of its signified components.

Consciousness an end to the means.

Intelligence

Intelligence is actually style, an individual's method of operation, his approach. Intelligence is the connections one chooses to make by virtue of one's personality or being, one's disposition towards certain choices. These connections are made within whatever body of knowledge an individual happens to possess.

It is as if intelligence were independent of what we normally consider 'intelligence' because it operates by stepping out of the way of data and letting that data arrange itself by its own apparent structure. The height of intelligence is the ability to disappear, to get out of the way.

simultaneous   multiple   indivisible

Hypercognition

When a poem is read, a painting shown or a theorem presented, an audience is exposed in a very short period of time to a structure which required much more time to fabricate. The actual compositional time in a work of art or a thesis is the sum of conceptualization & ideation that went into its composition. Thus when a poem is read back the actual assembly time informs the work with a sort of charge of temporality. Any such work of mind, be it poetry or mathematics, represents compressed cognitive time, its re-presentation is in effect time dilation.

It is a natural ability of consciousness to acquire information at a higher rate than it takes to produce it. The nervous system, by comprehending compressed cognitive sequences in real time, is performing well beyond its theoretical limitations in a mode which can be referred to as hypercognition. By exposing oneself to hypercognition, one, in effect, gradually acquires an artificial faculty, which is the basis of education.

Hypercognition, by definition, exists primarily in engram sequences, as memory. As a special condition of extemporization, of real-time cognition, it can only be sustained for brief periods of time.

In a word the idea.

Consciousness as User Friendly

Consciousness is the result of a highly suggestible, on-board processing unit. It is completely user friendly & can be accessed without complicated commands simply by human will.

The will to power is total user friendliness.

The power to will is an epiphenomenon of neural functioning.

Cross-Modal Transfer

Cross-modal association is the ability to apprehend an object with one sense and transpose its qualities into another. For example, an object seen can be later identified in darkness by touch alone. This ability to operate with internal models is felt by Eccles to be synonymous with imagination.

In 1967 Teuber proposed that language mediated the operation of a "central mechanism" which "transcended the divisions between the different senses". He postulated that language was a "supramodal" category "imposed upon experience" whose operative mode was synesthetic. "Language frees us from the tyranny of the senses." In 1965, Geschwind said that cross-modal association was "prerequisite" for language.

Cross-Modal Apprehensility

In mammals, body-parts other than hands are spoken of as prehensile if they can be used, like hands, for grasping or manipulating the environment. Certain species of monkey have prehensile tails which they use to assist in their arboreal acrobatics. What differentiates humans from primates is an *embodied prehensility* which inhabits the entire voluntary body. (Tactility is enhanced by flesh permeated with voluntary motor & somatic sensory nerve endings. A higher density facilitates greater sensitivity. This invagination is in direct proportional alliance with the higher integrative function; *i.e.,* consciousness). Our highly developed voluntary control, a somatic abstraction of sorts, is the flip-side of high level symbolic thought which characterizes human consciousness. We apprehend the world tactually, kinesthetically, through cross-modal transfer, by manipulating internal models of our environment.

Tools are materialized prehensilization. Ultimately the entire environment is prehensilized by consciousness. It becomes pregnant with incipient tool options, potentiating a vast array of possibilities in the world.

The Ideity

The ingredients of our days are not the houses, or mountains or even the persons around us, but are the looks, feels and sounds etc. that are of such objects.

— (Woodger, 1952)

The large associational component of both perception and memory seems to rely in great part on cross-modal input that re-affirms the signals from differing senses. *E.g.,* the smell of the memory situation, the light, the sound and mood *etc.* all compete at various levels for 'attention'. We could expect one sense to be 'tagged' by another at the time of perception and particularly at the point of recall, as an accessing device. "That smell reminds me of...."

This synesthetic 'tagging' of sensory input would provide a mnemonic addressing system that would be largely associational in operation. The capacity for subtle variation amongst individual associational-systems could easily account for the diversity of human personality. The singular identity, the 'I' perceived, the psyche or ego, is composed of a specific associational train, a tendency towards a singular sequencing of association. The individual is perceived by his/her 'method'. 'I' is an associational system, a group of symbols accreted around a singular causal continuity, *i.e. being,* which themselves constitute a meta-symbol, a synthesis equivalent to 'self'.

Consciousness is a neuronally imbedded associative identity.

Assume(d) the unspoken.

The Recombinant Fountain of Memory

Memory is stored, physiologically, throughout the entire cortex much as a hologram is stored on a piece of holographic film.* No matter how many times a hologram is divided, each small piece will still act as a window onto the whole image. Holographic memory, perfusing the mechanism of mind on both the noetic & physical planes, is the basis of mind/being.

According to Dr Wilder Penfield there is a section of the brain called the interpretive cortex which is devoted to the interpretation of present experience in the light of past experience. Because human thought is characterized by analogical mapping (the comparison of previously encoded material with present phenomena) the entire cerebral cortex can be usefully regarded as an interpretive cortex.

It is as if the syntax of action, the translation of will, is accomplished through a kind of grammar of experience. The components of this grammar, the individual bits of memory which constitute the vast store of our experiential memory, are selected and recombined into meaningful variations in the elucidation of will.

The constant upwelling of memory from the perfused mind or memory table is being.

The recombinant fountain of memory is will.

Purpose is wholly dependent on the *continuing* formation of memory.

*K.H. Pibram's analogy.

27

The Triune Brain

According to Joseph Altman's theory of the triune brain there are three levels of mentation. Each successive level of mentation represents a higher evolutionary modification. Thus the most primitive level, or reptilian brain, is called the *paleocephalon* and corresponds physiologically with the higher brain stem and the limbic systems. It engages in *pathic* thought and is the seat of emotion, motivation and the mechanism of consciousness. The second level, or mammalian brain, is called the *neencephalon,* and corresponds physiologically with the minor or right hemisphere of the cerebral cortex. It engages in *iconic* thought, that is to say it deals with symbolic representations of the environment and formulates appropriate responses by matching experience with memory. Its actions can be characterized more as habitual than deliberate. The most sophisticated and evolutionarily the most recent modification is the human mind, the *anthropocephalon* or dominant hemisphere. It engages in *noetic* thought, that is to say language and high-level symbolism, human consciousness.

However simplified, this model also touches on two very important notions in neuroanatomy, those of dominance and the two hemispheres of the brain. What is important about Altman's system is that it differentiates the right hemisphere from the left on the basis of its lack of humanity, that is to say, he locates human consciousness specifically in the left hemisphere of the brain. This attribute is reinforced by the simple procedure of injecting a solution of sodium amytal into the carotid artery which supplies either hemisphere. If it is injected into the right hemisphere the subject will be conscious although he or she will fail certain visual/spatial tests. If the sodium amytal is injected into the left hemisphere the subject will lose consciousness.

Hierarchic Levels of Mentation
(after Altman)

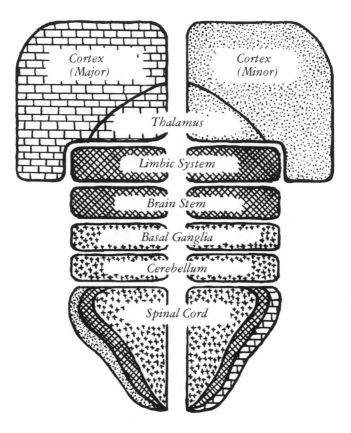

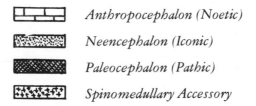

Anthropocephalon (Noetic)

Neencephalon (Iconic)

Paleocephalon (Pathic)

Spinomedullary Accessory

Anthropocephalon as *Stepping Razor*

The rapid onset, evolutionarily speaking, of ideation and language in our species explains perhaps the seemingly expedient manner in which these functions were lateralized in the brain. The functional asymmetry represented by hemispheric dominance marks a radical break with the previous evolutionary tradition of bilaterality.

The exigent adaptation of biological material to noetic purpose.

Stepping Razor is the title of a song by Jamaican reggae singer Peter Tosh. In the movie *Rockers* this song was the soundtrack for the visual documentation of several Jamaican Rastafarians walking. Their highly individualized gaits embodied an idiosyncratic & asymmetrical style, a contrapuntal walking dance which accentuated their lateral asymmetry.

Stepping razor is the acknowledged turbulence of lateralization.

Experiencing the Material Basis of Mind

A seizure is a storm in the brain, starting in one area and spreading through the cortex. The progression of a seizure from the focal point to the rest of the brain is called a Jacksonian March. Sometimes it will begin with a twitching finger, then hand, then forearm, then the whole arm, *etc.* Often, prior to a seizure the individual will experience an aura, similar in its effects to some of the more profound alterations produced by the hallucinogenic drugs.

At the beginning of a *grand mal* seizure there is a characteristic moaning cry of despair, a brain scream. Usually it is the first external signal of an impending seizure for bystanders, and it is not easily forgotten by them. Through it they vicariously experience the involuntary rupture of consciousness into pure neurological disorder.

There are certain types of migraines which border on epilepsy and which may not even produce a headache, and yet will profoundly alter the highest integrative mechanism. These migraines can manifest themselves as forced thinking, where the individual helplessly witnesses a series of strange & disturbing ideas stream through his or her mind. Other migraines can produce numbness in limbs, scintillating lights, pointillist & mosaic vision, *déjà vu* & forced reminiscences. All of these are temporary windows into the neurological substratum of consciousness.

A type of seizure can even be brought on experimentally. This is achieved by using an electroencephalogram to pick up the brain waves of an individual & then synchronizing a stroboscopic flash with them. In a sense it is a form of neurological feedback, where the basic rhythm of consciousness is fed back to itself. This technique will sometimes cause seizures even in individuals with no prior history of epilepsy. Even if one doesn't experience a seizure it is extremely uncomfortable for it literally deconstructs consciousness. One feels as if one is about to lose one's mind in the midst of a spastic & uncontrollable dread. It is consciousness desperately struggling to witness itself in the act of its own disintegration, a frightening fall infinitely repeated through the exploded armature of the mind.

Metaconsciousness

Human consciousness is a transcendentally homeostatic epiphenomenon, a self-regulating illusion tantamount to virtual existence. An aberration of previous evolutionary modes, it is purely a consequence of neural sophistication. A critical mass of neurons imbedded in a perceptual matrix.

Metaconsciousness is self-consciousness which by a kind of eversion has integrated with the universal mind.

The distance between noetic consciousness & metaconsciousness is revelation.

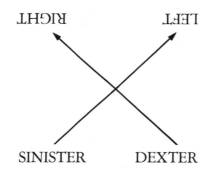

THE HERALDIC SUBJECTIVE

The Mirror

Let us say then that a mirror is a temporary position, a whistle-stop, between the "dog's buddha nature" and metaconsciousness.
The mirror was the first thing as fast as consciousness.

Consciousness an end means to the.

Attacus Atlas

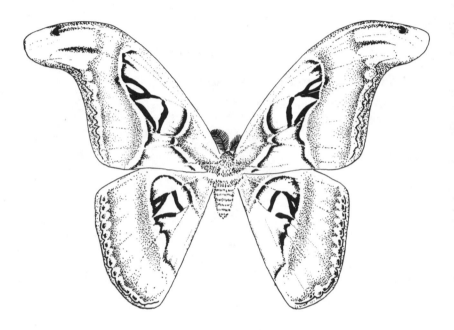

Insect Mimicry as a Thin Point

In the eyespots of giant moths predators see other predators fearful to them. The opening wings of the moth blossom into an hallucination of danger.

A reptile has had its profile painted by selective evolution on the wing-tips of the Atlas moth. This image is the index fear of a particular insectivore. A racial terror developed in the genetically sensitized emulsion of the moth's wings.

Incidental that the image of the reptile is translated into the genetic coding of another species. Not incidental that a perception beyond vision, an aperture opened by ancestral fear, becomes a slow invisible mirror held by the moth during the indelible cosmetics of its transformation.

Images of flowers, foliage, bark & animals are transferred between species, a commodity exchange of survival.

We are in-formed.

In background mimicry the forest sees itself. A mean foliage abstracted as only bilateral symmetry can. Whenever a representation is translated through the genetic aperture of survival into the vanishing point of the plane of symmetry, which is DNA, to materialize again as a generation of the plane of symmetry, we can call this representation a *thin point*. A thin point is a privileged view onto the immanent structure of reality & for this reason is a very efficient subject for visual flooding.

An image which has passed through the plane of symmetry is only one example of a thin point. There are other occurrences reached through very different mechanisms & mediums.

For us, protection from predators is an incidental function of mimicry.

Edge Features

Our vision relies on discontinuity & change. It seems the majority of neural processing in the striate cortex consists of an analysis of edge-features. An object is perceived by its edges, the relationship of discontinuous lines. All written languages are the abstraction and distillation of only the essential edge-features necessary to perceive the form on which meaning is concomitant.

Visual Flooding

Visual flooding is a nascent propensity of vision which can be utilized with little training. It is employed in the simultaneous assimilation of large areas of movement or complex patterns by staring fixedly at a central point in the field of attention. The discipline of this process consists in not allowing the peripheral blank-out that usually develops with a 'non-conscious' stare and in refraining from any internal monologue or film-of-images during meditation. This procedure is actually a type of reflexive perceptual hypnosis where the fovea centralis, the point of attention in the retina, is slowly expanded to sensitize the entire retina. The disengagement of self-awareness during the process of visual flooding facilitates direct access to the visual cortex without conscious interpolation, like a tourist without a camera. The essence of the phenomenon is imprinted directly into the experiential reservoir of the mind.

For richness of detail natural terrain is second to none for high-speed, complex integration. Any natural tableau or process, be it an insect, flowing water, house plants or a forest, is unmatched for infinite variation & three-dimensional detail down to microscopic level. It expedites matters if the subject of visual flooding hasn't been memorized or is constantly changing. Japanese rock & moss gardens are designed with specifically this purpose in mind, the best of which override a confrontation between limited terrain & habituation.

Visual flooding with a cloud chamber, a glass apparatus filled with mist in which atomic particles leave white trails, will imprint the physics of quantum reality as direct experience. When one can exist totally between the materialization of a particle track and its decay then one can slowly expand fovea centralis until all the tracks in the cloud chamber are registered simultaneously in a harmony as self evident & resplendent as the stars.

Visual flooding can be successfully practiced on a single-trace oscilloscope while it reproduces music.

Visual flooding is a basic operating skill of video games.

Each variation of the species is an instruction.

Paravisual Flooding—Border Zone Excitation

The visual field is a highly charged artifact of neurological integration. What you are looking at, your field of vision, is simultaneously 'projected' in the occipital lobe of the brain, mapped almost 1 for 1 onto the 3mm. thick 'screen' of the striate cortex. The visual field represents a discrete area of the cerebral cortex which is externalized. An invisible vertical juncture demarcates the seamless optical confluence of left and right hemispheres. The region beyond or 'behind' peripheral vision represents adjacent functional areas of the cortex.

By regarding the periphery of vision as a neural boundary and not an optical one it is possible to grasp the neurological basis of vision. By simultaneously flattening the depth & heightening the curvature of the field of vision it is possible to interpret the visual field as the externalized 'clear' portion of the larger sphere of the entire cerebral cortex. When the field of vision is *experienced* as equivalent to the surface of the cerebral cortex then simply by staring fixedly ahead, so as to secure an unchanging/undistracting scene, one can attempt a noetic deconstruction of conditioned visual experience. At this point, without moving your eyes, you move only your *focus* of attention, like a mobile fovea centralis, from the centre towards the periphery of vision. You can then move this 'cursor', the phantom fovea, towards and past the edge of peripheral vision.

At this point you will have a 'visually' localized point of excitation in a region of the cerebral cortex adjacent to the visual cortex. If you directed the cursor through the bottom of your peripheral vision it would correlate with the top of the striate cortex and would intersect the parietal lobes and the visual associative areas of the adjacent temporal lobes. A definite effect of border zone excitation of the parietal lobe would be tangible & peculiar alterations of perceived body proportions and position.

Successful paravisual flooding would represent a breakthrough of noetic localization, the direct excitation of the cortex contrary to the normal associative pathways of the brain. It would be in effect a metaviolation of consciousness, a second order of noetic mind operating within the physical substratum of the iconic mind. As such it would represent a profound synesthesia, akin to the direct electric stimulation of the exposed cortex.

Masturbation, with a noetic model providing stimulation, is directly ancestral to this technique. The feedback of alpha rhythms through electroencephalographic stroboscopic synchronization is a technological application of a similar principle, stimulation contrary to normal excitation by using the brain against itself.

Paravisual flooding is the primary stage of the first real expansion of consciousness.

The Cerebral Cortex
View of Anthropocephalon or Dominant/Left Hemisphere

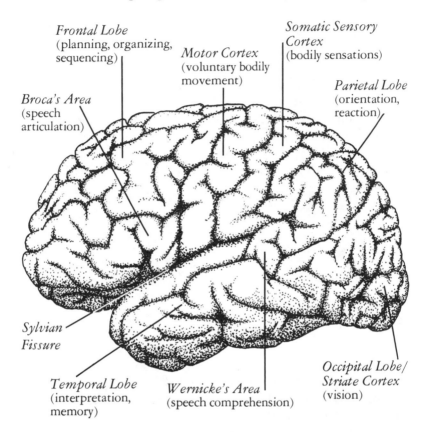

Frontal Lobe
(planning, organizing, sequencing)

Motor Cortex
(voluntary bodily movement)

Somatic Sensory Cortex
(bodily sensations)

Parietal Lobe
(orientation, reaction)

Broca's Area
(speech articulation)

Sylvian Fissure

Temporal Lobe
(interpretation, memory)

Wernicke's Area
(speech comprehension)

Occipital Lobe/ Striate Cortex
(vision)

Explanation

The cerebral (or neocortex) is a 3 mm thick layer of 10^{10} neurons & represents the highest data processing region of the brain. Unfolded, its surface area is approximately 1.5 sq. ft. (Space efficiency and natal head size have necessitated complex folding.) The two hemispheres communicate via the *corpus collosum* & their various functional areas communicate via the higher brain stem. Recent investigations of the *striate cortex* suggest that the neocortex is subdivided into almost mathematically aligned microprocessing units (consisting of approximately 10,000 neurons each) called *hypercolumns* (Frisby) or *modules* (Eccles).

Intensifying Consciousness

Knowledge is power. Individual knowledge is individual power (*i.e.,* individual 'secret' knowledge uncommunicated to others). The potential energy of uncommunicated secret knowledge held by an individual increases proportionately to the social pertinency of that knowledge. Even irrelevant knowledge, if uncommunicated, increases the personal power of the individual. Saying disperses the energy. "He who talks does not know."

Acquired Skills

Acquired skills enable us to transcend biological limitations. Typing sixty words a minute on a typewriter requires a performance well beyond the minimum human decision time of one-half second. An apparently impossible feat. Acquired skills are ontogenically assumed tools imprinted into the biological somatic totality of a human being. By increasing the adaptive repertoire of man they represent precursors of an auxiliary, artificial intelligence. The communal repertoire of human skills, enriched by individual discovery, expands as it is transmitted through successive generations. In essence, we are the sum of our acquired skills, themselves the inheritance of our noetic phylogeny.

The superman is already amongst us.

The Ghost in the Machine—Proprioceptive Prosthetics

A human being can inhabit a machine. The somatic percept, one's kinesthetic self-representation, is extensile. It can flow, proprioceptively, like a phantom nervous system, into the fabric of a machine, be it tool or vehicle. This is the point at which one says one has the 'feel' of it. The machine is permeable to the 'charge' of consciousness because it is an appropriate vehicle for the will. This is tantamount to the psychic possession of mass.

Shadow of consciousness superimposed in the molecular structure of tools.

We are the ghost in the machine.

Proprioceptive Learning

Who feels it knows it.
— Jamaican aphorism

Newtonian physics is our matrix, we experience its tactile causality in door-handles and vehicles. The equation is unnecessary to throw a stone. Computers will facilitate our tactile absorption of quantum mechanics. Mathematics our phantom mind.

Interface Prosthetics

The interface between human and tool prostheticizes both the human and the tool. Only the stump of a foot is necessary to press an accelerator, or the bulge of a shoulder to hold a telephone against the ear.

A dime will serve as a screwdriver.

Tools

Anything contrived by the hand of man, an artifact, has an infernal glitter to it, almost a dark luminosity. Tools have an intense luminous darkness to them, an incisionary almost inhuman wisdom. In an autosignification of purpose a tool's singular task is differentiated from its matrix by the tool itself, an instrument of purpose.

The tool *is* purpose.

Vice-grips

The vice-grip is a multi-purpose tool, extremely flexible as an implement of will. It is, in fact, a thin-point or signature for the world (boreal techno-culture). It is a charmed arbiter, a unit of meaning in the natural history of our synthetic matrix. The little metaphor for the human, a flexible organism which effectively mutates to facilitate structural coupling to whichever interface it must adjust. It becomes a precursor of artificial intelligence. Its generalized purpose allows it to adapt to continuously changing circumstances, it is the pivot on which structural plasticity, engendered by entropy and evolution, articulates.

Invention

Every invention has been a case of instant gratification. We were satisfied with exactly what was necessary (and *only* what was necessary) to span the gap between desire & actuality. An iron bridge is the actualization of desire. It is the nature of this gratification to close the door on each solution.

A discovery obscures further tangents.

Artificial intelligence is a continuous instant of gratification.

Concrete Technical Reality

One of the single most dominant characteristics of human technology is its aura of provisionality. Even a highly finished object, such as a commercial automobile, is a provisional structure with interchangeable parts that can be improvised if the necessity arises. A lot of engineering solutions, particularly those which need to function dependably under constant usage, as in urban transit situations, have an aura of provisionality. Many of these devices appear crude to a mathematical or ideal sensibility habituated to elegant solutions.

Utility in high demand areas seems to exact mechanical solutions which seem primitive or crude looking, even if they are the acme of functional engineering. This is exemplified in those areas of our transportation technology where three-dimensional objects interact with virtually two-dimensional grids, such as train tracks & street-car power cables. These seem to be weak points of provisionality, almost unduly vulnerable. They are somehow at the nexus of deterministic causal constraints, functional solutions which are contingent on the physical nature of the universe, its laws, the mechanics of our reality. It is as if the interface of our technology with these laws generates a kind of heightened provisional ambience which is at once a solution to, and a codex of, our relation to the cosmos.

Tools, or devices designed to maintain or perform operations on other devices have this quality also, though it is complicated by an invidious anthropomorphization of intent.

For example, street-cars all come down to a strangely expedient & clumsy looking tongue and groove relation between the aeriel power line and the pole assembly. Train tracks, following the constraints of their planar reality, must negotiate complex & laborious looking complexes of switches & cross-overs. It is as if the constraints of physical reality conspire with expedience, necessity, to produce a natural history of entrenched genericism within a finite array of mechanical solutions.

Increasing control of previously uncontrolled events is the aim of noetic evolution.

Representation is subjectively perceived as a form of control.

Aural Space as Equivalent to Quantum Reality

Aural space is divine space because it most nearly parallels divine or celestial consciousness. Celestial consciousness is similar to Pascal's definition of Nature, "an infinite sphere, whose center is everywhere and whose circumference is nowhere". Aural space is so curved that if the hypothetical listener is sensitive enough nothing is hidden from him. One cannot see opposite sides of the same object but one can *hear* them.

Aural space is a perceptual allegory for quantum reality in which the fabric of the universe is behaviourally equivalent to virtually massless interpenetrating jellies unified into one continuous electromagnetic gel.

Discarnate Territoriality

Every human has a minimal operational territory, an invisible social field surrounding each individual which is subconsciously acknowledged by others. This territory is quantitatively flexible, diminishing in crowds & expanding in open spaces. During hostile or aggressive confrontations this field becomes critical, a transgression resulting in violence or retreat.

The telephone cuts across all territorial conventions during hostile or aggressive interactions. We are confronted with a totally novel situation (phylogenically) when a discarnate aggressor, often a credit manager from the local exchange, not only trespasses personal territory but proceeds with overt verbal aggression past the point at which adrenalin levels would normally precipitate physical violence. The skilled aggressor can easily out-manoeuvre the flustered & helpless rage of his or her victim.

Lateral Mobility

The leisure class consists of two levels of income. The distance between these two levels is the mean income of the middle class. As the leisure class is defined by iconographic taste & disposable time a couple with no dependants or 'singles' without a mortgage can easily gravitate towards the social vortex of the leisure class, whereas the lower middle class, even with a higher disposable income, is barred by harsh economic necessity. We have the odd situation where the middle class can enter a 'higher' social class by disposing of its assets.

Food

Food debases the free-trade zone because essentially it is invaluable. People will & must pay anything for it. Anorexia nervosa is the 'pleasure' of the leisure class.

Sensory By-Pass

Sensory by-passing is now possible. Dr John Girvin of University Hospital, London, Ontario has successfully implanted an electrode array in the striate cortex of a blind person which converts visual signals from a camera into a phosphene display. This device is referred to as a visual prosthesis.

Olfaction is a sensory by-pass of sorts. Unlike the other senses whose tracts are routed through the thalamus in the upper brain stem, the olfactory projections proceed directly to the cortex. This is the only instance of unmediated sensory data impinging directly on cortical neurons. The associative mechanism of smell, in terms of cross-modal transfer, must be qualitatively different from the other senses. The hallucination of smells, for example, would be just an idea.

The textured frequencies of music could be patched-in directly to the central nervous system with no appreciable loss of structure. By over-riding local reflex arcs a dancer's musculature could be choreographed into an involuntary series of exquisite, digitalized movements, a direct-to-dance transformation of the original signal.

The by-pass conversation would be held entirely in connotation.

Language

Language is the gauge of our provisional reality, the standardized description of a constantly variable world. It is the point of consciousness at the still centre of time, even if the discharge of reference takes place cumulatively at the end of each sentence. We literally make it up as we go along, use its infinite array of permutations to suit any situation. Its usefulness comes from its formlessness, the subtle interchangeability of its components in order to conform to descriptions of unanticipated phenomena. Its utility lies in its extreme lack of identity, its expertise in indicating but never being something, its immateriality.

Language, in order to function optimally, must be in essence the opposite of identity, in order to adapt to the eternal present of both temporal causality & consciousness. Consciousness, although modelled on causality, is actually timeless. Language, particularly as it is manifested in the interior monologue, is the only thing that can keep as still as consciousness, a simulacrum of consciousness, which is why it seduces the individual into identifying it as synonymous with consciousness.

It is the swimmer who swims against the flow of the river, who remains stationary relative to the bank. It is a geosynchronous satellite reflecting a paradigm of consciousness back to the observer on earth.

The Living Language

Orchestration of a nervous system which contains $10''$ neurons in the brain alone requires a high-level integrative mechanism. Consciousness is this mechanism. Consciousness was a direct consequence of neural complexity. At some point on the road from *Homo erectus* to *Homo sapiens* the neuronal mass of the cortex went critical and noetic consciousness was achieved. Communication between members of a species which has attained this consciousness requires a complex symbolic system of reference. Language is such a system.

Language has been a cumulative project of *Homo sapiens* and to a certain extent before him, *Homo erectus*. As in other cumulative projects undertaken by our species, such as the selective hybridization of domestic animals, its ontogeny exceeds the life-span of the individual. However, language has had a much more profound effect on its creators than has the hybridization of domestic animals. Once conceived, language became self-replicating, a lexical organism imbedded in the species. The evolution of language, inextricably bound with the evolution of our consciousness as a species, has diverged from its parallel status and taken on a life of its own. Language is virtually an independent intelligence utilizing humans as neural components in a vast and inconceivable sentience.

The living language exists symbiotically with the human 'host'.

Language is this mechanism.

The House of the Living Language

At birth the human brain is largely hard-wired; the striate cortex is 'programmed' for vision and the motor cortex can already direct purposeful movement. There are other parts of the brain which are not hard-wired however. Primary amongst these is the future speech centre. The speech centre is imprinted through the acquisition of whichever language a child is born into.

As the child learns a language, the speech centres are 'programmed' by the living language in a sort of post-natal embryology. Through an attritional process, in which redundant neural pathways atrophy through lack of use, the speech centres are imprinted with the abstract circuitry of language. The living language arranges its 'house' with sure and precise hands. There is recent evidence that the physical localization of discrete functions, such as musical ability, are affected by whichever language is acquired in infancy. Language acquisition is in effect the beach-head of a process in which, eventually, the whole of an individual's consciousness is conceptually biased by language.

Language can be regarded as a psychic parasite which has genetically earmarked a section of the cortex for its own accommodation.

The Adjective Gate

The dictionary defines language by cross referencing. Language is defined in terms of itself, it is a recursive system, an almost magic self-referential mechanism into which the child gains entry through nouns. Nouns are the first words of choice for the language novice because they are associated by example with objects.

In the primal grammar of the two-year old the rules of syntax and construction are extremely different from mature grammar. There is a 'proto-grammar' of sorts, which is first constellated around the *primal nouns*. Because complete expression of the human individual requires instruments of desire and control, the primal noun exhibits verbal qualities as well. A child will use a noun to imply an action, or as an imperative.

The language novice discovers the self-referential nature of adult language when the first adjectives are used, primarily as fine-tuners of nouns. Adjectives, as qualities of the 'things' (nouns), become the harbingers of the precision signifier, an illusion of infinite customization of signifiers to match 'the signified', enabling an exact description.

After the acquisition of adjectives and adverbs (which are almost interchangeable in the primal grammar), the primal noun undergoes fission and splits into a verb and noun proper. The verb becomes a rarefaction, a purification of the modalities of desire and control and eventually, description, and their most appropriate vehicle. The primal noun loses some of its charge in the process.

Adjectives are structural necessities of the language mechanism which, in a sort of meta-tautology, set the entire system in motion, in both the acquisitional process and in the day to day functioning of the living language. For the child they are the gate into the recursive matrix, the initiators of the lexicon.

We are all Helen Kellers

Language is a closed system to which we all miraculously gain admission. We begin as linguistic deaf-mutes. (This gives rise to some of our earliest existential performance anxieties, irrevocably intertwined into the primal language experience.) And like Helen Keller we all acquired that first miraculous noun, made the ultimate connection, in the water-pump of adult semiotics. The fact that we are evolutionarily designed to make that connection doesn't lessen the miracle of its occasion. The noun is the magic sign, the charmed referent which admits us into the human language.

That a word sequence could ultimately express the needs & observations of an individual is a miracle. Communication is a string of incredible coincidences.

A most inimical host.

Grammar as Swiss Army Knife

The basic combinatorial rules of language are more critical than the lexicon itself. The average adult possesses a more exact grammatical knowledge of a given language than he or she does of the total possible vocabulary of that language. Grammar is a constant armature which manipulates the variables of language into the most appropriate form.

Each word change the word.

The Irrefutable Argument

Music is a side-effect, an artifact of consciousness. It is the arrangement of frequencies and rhythms in a manner which appears meaningful to the nervous system. It is a libidinal language received sympathetically by consciousness in much the same manner that haemoglobin prefers to bond with carbon monoxide over oxygen. By mimicking afferent signals it produces something like an enzyme recognition failure.

A synesthetic precursor of syntax, it is a virtual argument without refutation.

If such can be said to be said.

The Word Store as Planar Thesaurus

If we look upon the 'intent' of an idea, as it manifests itself in words, we see an original impulse which elaborates itself in a tree-structure from the general to the specific.

Individual words are chosen out of a group of synonyms. Clusters of synonyms become target areas of meaning superimposed on a kind of *planar thesaurus* existing as an engram in the cortex. A synonym cluster can be visualized as a circle or gradient of specificity, as meaning-correspondence diffuses outwards from the target or 'ideal' in an areola of increasingly less synonymous terms. A storage system relying on proximal clusters of synonyms would produce errors of speech like, "Rush hour looks *franatic* tonight," where the differentiation between the almost synonymous terms "frenetic" and "frantic" is so slight that articulation would proceed before the final choice between the terms had been completed.

If we regard pre-verbalized intent as a storm cloud hovering over the planar thesaurus, then lightning will serve to illustrate both tree-structure and the direction of impulse. The charge, flowing from intent to articulation, begins as a main leader (the drift of it) then branches out into specific signifiers/referents which act as conductors, grounding the charge through the points of least resistance to the intent.

By reproducing the analogy of lightning on paper, placing intent at the top and the target sequence at the bottom, we arrive at a structure that bears a remarkable resemblance to generative transformational grammar's deep structure trees. This resemblance is shown on pages 69 & 70.

Syntax, the *sequence* of target synonyms, can be said to be configured largely by sequential prediction or the superimposed and inherent logic of the house of the living language, the linguistic cortex. Neuroanatomically we would expect two functional areas of localization, one area which would access and store synonymous clusters, the planar thesaurus, and another area which would pre-articulate the target synonyms in a meaningful sequence. This order is determined by the living language.

Meaning is the return stroke.

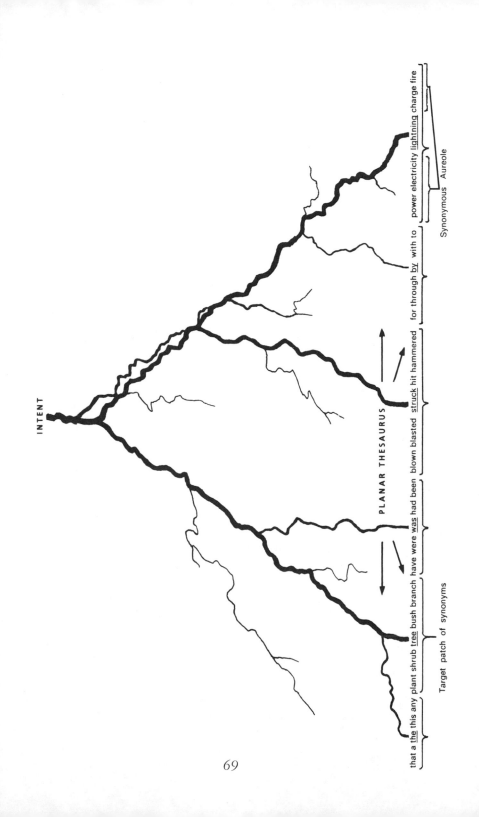

INTENT

PLANAR THESAURUS

that a the this any plant shrub tree bush branch have were was had been blown blasted struck hit hammered for through by with to power electricity lightning charge fire

Target patch of synonyms

Synonymous Aureole

GENERATIVE TRANSFORMATIONAL DEEP STRUCTURE

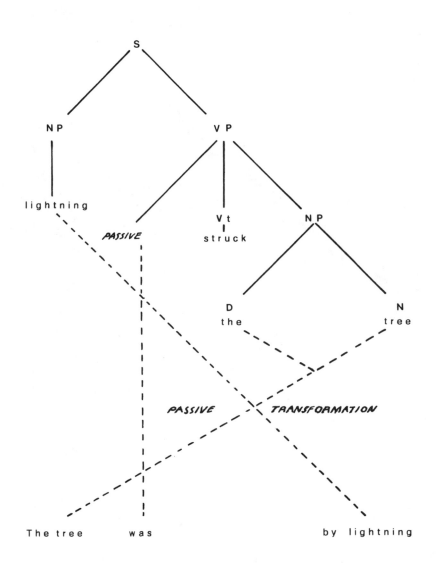

The tree was struck by lightning.

Associational Areola as Grid Erectile

The idealized specific, the word, is served by the diffuse, the nervous system relying on numerous distinct channels each carrying a slightly different feature of the information.

The Planar Thesaurus or word store, is operated on as a surface. Intent, acting through a plane parallel to this surface, is a charged localization which attracts appropriate referents and repels inappropriate ones. The associational cluster takes on a nipple-like structure in the presence of a charged intent, the appropriate terms vying at the tip of the nipple and the less appropriate ones sloping away towards the perimeter of the areola.

The entire nipple and areola however, can be stimulated, aroused if you like, through the use of a procedural system which breaks down referential specificity, such as poetry. This generalized excitation and erectile swelling of the whole nipple and areola de-focalizes intent which concurrently has increased access to unique and un-habituated associative sequences.

This procedure maximizes the inherent multichanneled capabilities of the nervous system.

Border Zone Excitation

The associational areola is contiguous with surrounding areolas such that the 'nipples' are adrift in an areolar ocean. This ocean does not change in character until it encounters another functional area, say the border-zone between the visual and linguistic cortexes.

Erogenized border-zone areoles would generate true functional synesthesia. Blurring and exciting border-zones to produce hybrid percepts, they would act to increase the performance envelope of specific functional areas.

Hypercognitive sequences would be a natural by-product of border zone excitation.

Homonyms as linguistic Necker Cubes

The homonym, where a word's sign is identical to another of different meaning, can be regarded as the linguistic equivalent of an optical illusion, specifically Necker Cubes. In Necker Cubes the viewer's interpretations of identical sensory input alternate between two contradictory modes of perspective. The homonym, like the Necker Cube, alternates between two interpretations, two significations of an identical sensory input.

Ambiguity in poetry can be said to rely on the same 'perceptual breakdown' that takes place with optical illusions, as the interpretive charge of poetry is higher than 'general usage'.

Connotation is the fine edge of the homonymic wedge.

Writing

A work of literature is revealed to its author much as if it were a hidden order of nature. Once begun, the natural trajectory of a written train of thought elaborates an implicit order. The first sentence carries within it the blueprint for the whole subsequent work, much as an embryo contains the code for the adult organism. The inexorable systemic permutations, the intrinsic logic of la langue, fused on a deep & archetypal level with the author's individual style, becomes its own strategy of propagation, of crystalline accretion. The solution out of which these linguistic crystals precipitate is human consciousness.

The whole of a work of literature can be inferred from its parts as the parts can be inferred from the whole.

Unlike an uncovered law, however, the progeny of the original sentence can mutate & return to the site of their inception to alter it, like an endlessly self-manipulative teleology. Not only is such the atemporal & incestuous nature of literature, but also the paradigm of consciousness itself.

Re-writes as the enactment of self-observation, the paradox of consciousness.

Metaphor Templates

By disengaging a metaphor from its original application and then applying it to a novel setting one can fast-breed hypercognitive structures. Conversely, by applying the laws of the metaphor throughout the systemic permutations of that metaphor; *e.g.,* if history is a book then limestone must be the pages of that book and fossils the writing on those pages etc., one can generate novel associative binaries throughout the 'field' of which the original metaphor is but a minor component.

By reversing the causal flow of analogy language becomes a procedural system for generating hypercognitive structures.

As if, like hopeless paranoids with delusions of reference, we couldn't help reading sense into any sequence of words due to the referential bias of language, and that this paranoia of reference is itself the engine of invention.

Legal Language as the Ultimate Signifier

A company, a corporate entity replete with merchandise, inventory, real-estate & personnel does not exist unless it exists on paper. Print validates its reality. Consider the phrase "put that in writing". Law is simply an extension of the authority of reference. Consider the phrases "to the letter of the law" or "throw the book at him". A lawyer "represents" you, is the living language personified, the incarnate scribe of your printed needs. A lawyer facilitates your translation into two-dimensionality, "puts you on paper".

Language is a cognitive prosthesis.

Fovea Centralis

A man is looking out of his eyes and is reading or talking. He gesticulates "expressively" while he talks, or his comment pencil glitters in the electric light. The frequency of his nervous movements becomes continuous, his hands begin to occupy space through movement. The solid form that is inhabited by his hands pulsates, forms a ring, a tunnel around his vision. The solid is composed of movement and is dangerous, his eyes wander, verging on sleep or hypnosis.

Dreams

Dreams are the basal portions, the wave roots of daytime thoughts, the undertow of diurnal anxieties or joys. It is as if the interplay of desire and apprehension in the cortex was like the visible portion of waves on a lake and the deeper, rolling motion of the subsurface, benthic or underwater roots of the waves was like the emotive reflection of cortical thoughts in the limbic mind. As if the tree above ground disappeared and the roots projected a phantom tree, its branches blowing in a nocturnal, paleocephalic wind.

Attention in Dreams

When one attends to a specific object in a dream—if, for instance, one picks up an object and looks directly at it, as one would ordinarily while awake—in 90% of the cases the object will begin to mutate and transform identity. This is an example of the mutative effects of signifying consciousness in dreams, within which context it is mutagenic, a reversal of the waking mode. Dreams are to be experienced primarily in a non-specific, diffuse or general way, their very *substance* degrades or breaks down under scrutiny. This mutation can be viewed as a model for the narrative engine within all dreams. The irritation of dream terrain by signifying consciousness "makes it happen".

Resonating Paleocephalic Loops

Memory can be emotionally 'tagged' in much the same way that a chemical substance can be tagged with a radioactive isotope in order to trace its movements. A memory which has been coloured by an emotion, emotionally 'tagged' *per se,* will resonate in the paleocephalon even in the absence of a cortical engram, a conscious thought, as a purely emotive resonating loop. This loop will remain activated by reward circuitry until a scanning process presents the correct match as a cortical engram. One might, for instance, be vaguely troubled by something and realize that one has forgotten a task which was, perhaps mildly unpleasant, but which was necessary to further self interest. At this point one would focus on the 'mood' while running a number of irritating candidates for the 'mood'. When the correct match is presented the disquieting loop is relieved.

Resonating paleocephalic loops, or sequences of them, could become 'locales' or perhaps even narrative shells in the context of dreams, when the anthropocephalon and neencephalon are disengaged by sleep.

Autonomic Dream Narratives

Serotonin is a neurotransmitter which mediates chemical signals in the brain. Its action on the thalamus, a structure in the upper brain stem, produces sleep. The molecular structure of serotonin is almost identical with that of the hallucinogenic drug psilocybin. Although their psychopharmacological effects differ it could be that they share an overlooked similarity, being that of suggestibility. Just as the individual who has ingested psilocybin is highly suggestible, particularly in the emotive domain, so is the dreamer highly suggestible to proprioceptive/autonomic inputs, the interior of the body.

Internal organs suggest the narratives of some dreams.

The Limbic System & Brain Stem

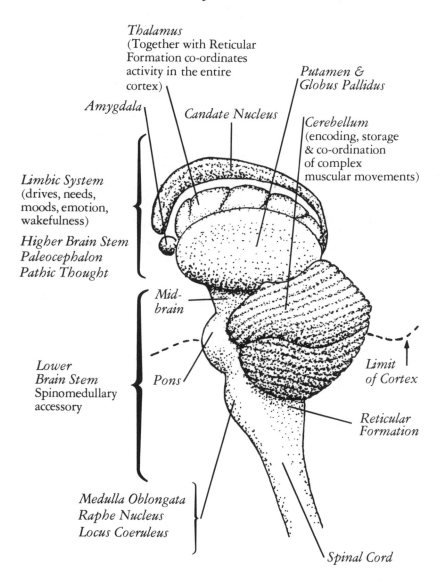

Thalamus
(Together with Reticular
Formation co-ordinates
activity in the entire
cortex)

Putamen &
Globus Pallidus

Amygdala

Candate Nucleus

Cerebellum
(encoding, storage
& co-ordination
of complex
muscular movements)

Limbic System
(drives, needs,
moods, emotion,
wakefulness)

Higher Brain Stem
Paleocephalon
Pathic Thought

Mid-
brain

Lower
Brain Stem
Spinomedullary
accessory

Pons

Limit
of Cortex

Reticular
Formation

Medulla Oblongata
Raphe Nucleus
Locus Coeruleus

Spinal Cord

A Topography of Psyche in Recurrent Dreams

Topography, representing either landscape or architecture, manifests itself in recurrent or serial dreams in two modes. In the first mode an actual or acquired topography is presented. This is usually based on a landscape or building familiar from childhood containing objects and locales which have their antecedents in objective reality. The second mode is a purely internal, symbolic topography which is independent of any actual geography. It is possible that this autogenically derived topography is archetypally transferable in the genetic code; *e.g.,* an architecture or recurrent landscape can be passed on in its basic format, genetically, through successive generations. As in all recurrent or serial dreams both the autogenic and the acquired landscapes recur, and can be visited in successive dreams in much the same manner that one can visit various locales of a given topography in the actual world.

An actual topography can also be acquired by adults with surprising alacrity. Sometimes a brief exposure will imprint a novel landscape into the dream archive. An acquisition of this nature suggests that the outline of the actual topography corresponds to, or is congruent with, a previously existing internal symbolic topography or 'map' which is easily transposed into an actual landscape. This indicates a spatio-temporal map within the cortex, an exotopic landscape perhaps existing physiologically like the map of the body in the motor cortex, which readily matches itself with the actual world, much like terrain recognition programs where a Cruise Missile is on course as long as it is above the terrain programmed into its memory circuits.

Narrative Shells in Recurrent Dreams

A feature common to recurrent dreams involving both the acquired and autogenic topographies is the *narrative shell*. A landscape forms a matrix in which are imbedded 'locales', each with a specific ambience, a 'mood' or 'flavour' which determines the nature of the 'plot' that is associated, or unfolds within, that locale. Each shell is an archetypal narrative.

The narrative shells are in close proximity to each other and a series of separate dreams or episodes linked in one night will often consist of the passage through several narrative shells. Episodes are determined by the 'path' through various shells.

One can negotiate the dream topography as in a familiar place and determine which narrative shells will be intersected, though decisions by the somnambulistic will seem to follow the path of least resistance in terms of yielding to emotional content. Emotion materializes the dreaded and beloved objects, the form and 'situation' of dreams.

Narrative shells are transparent, though occasionally their margins will shimmer in the exotopic landscape.

Dreams are pure intention.

Inhibitory Consciousness

...because of this inhibition a strong (tactile) stimulus is often surrounded by a cutaneous area that has reduced sensitivity.
— John C. Eccles

Waking consciousness is largely inhibitional. In perception inhibition negatively highlights specific incoming sensory signals by suppressing the activity of adjacent neural pathways. It is a causally linked enhancement of items significant to survival. This negative sculpting which surrounds an excitatory pathway is the same mechanism which produces the insensate areola in the epigraph above. In this mode consciousness could be said to *be* the action of suppressing extraneous data, on both the noetic & sensory levels, in order to enact will specifically, as causal reality demands. The inhibitional activity of the anthropo-cephalon reflects the overall operation of perception in general, a smoothing out of the jagged sensory continuum in order to facilitate the operation of a higher integrative function. The ideal specific of the immaculate perception is an extension of the same over-all operation of the nervous system.

Guinea pigs have been trained to discern smaller & smaller amounts of particular scents, finally being trained to detect the presence of literally a few molecules per million parts. This response to trace amounts of reactive chemicals, in terms of an animal's ever-increasing ability to react to them, is facilitated by inhibitory specificity. Rehearsal gradually hard-wires these changes at the cellular level.

Enhancement of receptor specificity by inhibition, *the* mechanism for maintaining causal isomorphism by the organism, entails an idealization which must, perforce, be *interpretive,* insofar as one *samples* (the natural limitation of our senses) a continuum. No matter how accurate an organism is in maintaining behaviour congruent with external reality it *must* be abstracted by its very mode of operation. This abstraction is physiologically underpinned by the .5 second antedating of experience by the cortex, the 're-setting' of the arrival of incoming sensory signals in order to make reaction coincide temporally with the event. This antedation is a miracle of sorts, a prayer answered every half second.

Inhibitory Consciousness & Dreams

Waking consciousness is encoded in the fluctuating & transient interplay of inhibitory & excitatory patterns in the brain. The experience of 'personality' in oneself and other humans would be evidence for trains of persistent anthropocephalic loops. These loops would manifest themselves electrically as standing waveforms. Indeed, electroencephalograms have detected just such individual differences. This is the unique adjustment of a neuro-electrical organism to reality which comprises individuality, and the focus of consciousness on this very causal reality 'unhinges' the anthropocephalon, or dominant cortex, from the limbic/paleocephalic substratum, the inner continuum, which motivates & flavours it.

At night, during sleep, selective inhibitory control is abandoned, and the anthropocephalon is first drugged, by the action of serotonin on the thalamus, and then flooded by resonating emotive loops arising from the paleocephalon. The anthropocephalon is then submerged in the phatic dialogues of the limbic system.

Casting our nets into the communolect.

Dreaming

The associational train which accompanies thought, the film of images, becomes dream when the need for organized conscious response is deleted by sleep. The reflective/associational train, when disengaged from monitoring the world, begins to key to internal stimuli. The film of images is still in a conscious 'mode'; however, it is no longer reflecting external reality.

Contralaterality in Dream and Verge of Sleep States

Dreams are perhaps the by-products of a reflexive, compensatory mirror flooding of opposite hemispheres. Possibly they are the companions of an equalization process, a concomitant of sleep, whereby localized functional areas of the two hemispheres are transferred contralaterally.

In dream or verge-of-sleep states our innate symmetrical bias may become a mechanism which releases the content of lateral functions into their opposite counterparts within the brain. The contralateral mixing of the language centres of the dominant hemisphere with the spatial/somatic orientation centres of the minor hemisphere might produce effects of perceived body size & proportions. This could well be the mechanism producing somatic distortions on the verge of sleep. The 'disengaged' anthropocephalon could be discharging phatic or involuntary linguistic constructions which would be montaged, overlayed on the perception of self in the contralateral parietal lobe. The perseverance of phantom dialogues, involuntary emissions of linguistic sequences, might well explain the high proportion of visual puns & symbology in dreams.

We know that conscious experience in dreams consists of an anthropocephalon still functioning almost bureaucratically in conscious mode, vainly aligning itself with an external waking reality from which it has been disengaged. It is as if the anthropocephalon were functioning in 'neutral' while possibly being flooded with the data of the contralateral hemisphere.

Perhaps specific functional regions of the mind, particularly those which are most stressed when awake, are de-activated, 'reduced' as it were, to the same status as the rest of the brain during sleep, as a necessary concomitant of the disengagement from a reality which those localizations manipulate. When, during sleep, a relative symmetry of function is attained, a kind of homeostasis, (itself perhaps a function of an innate bilateral/symmetrical bias), takes over and possibly begins to feed signals from one side of the brain to the other. Dreams could be viewed as a kind of noise, random interference patterns which are the by-product of the re-establishment of neuro-chemical homeostasis in the brain.

The Cerebral Cortex
(dorsal view, both hemispheres)

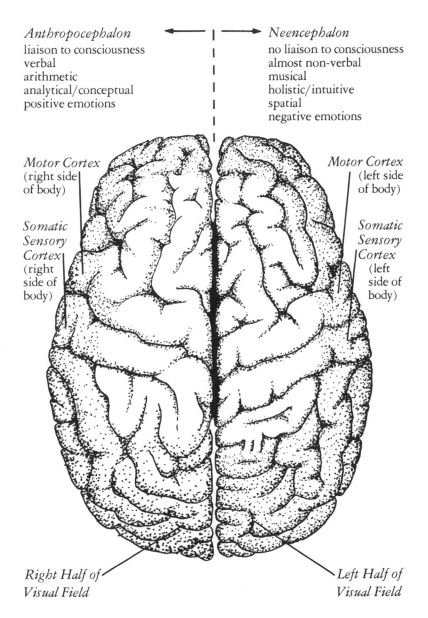

Anthropocephalon
liaison to consciousness
verbal
arithmetic
analytical/conceptual
positive emotions

Neencephalon
no liaison to consciousness
almost non-verbal
musical
holistic/intuitive
spatial
negative emotions

Motor Cortex
(right side
of body)

Motor Cortex
(left side
of body)

*Somatic
Sensory
Cortex*
(right
side of
body)

*Somatic
Sensory
Cortex*
(left
side of
body)

*Right Half of
Visual Field*

*Left Half of
Visual Field*

Dream Reification

Dream reification is conducted by materializing an object out of a dream. In the occasional dream there will be an object which you do not recognize but which you will remember in every detail upon waking. If you make a quick drawing of the object in the morning, with details of the size & modelling (for often these objects are sculptural), you can then reproduce it. The materialized dream object, placed in your living situation, will act as a context marker spanning two references or realms. Dream consciousness & waking consciousness.

Somatic Distortions at the Verge of Sleep

When one is on the verge of falling asleep one sometimes experiences peculiar feelings, odd disfigurements of bodily perception. A common sensation is the feeling of being very large or very tiny, of having lilliputian or brobdingnagian proportions. Other common affects are gross disproportions, such as having a huge head & jaws with very tiny teeth, or large hands & a small body.

It is possible that these sensations & others like them may be the direct apprehension of the somatotopic homunculus. In other words, the motor sensory cortex is being experienced directly by the conscious mind from within, so to speak, according to its own intrinsic ratios. Hypothetically this cross-modal percept could be a sort of short circuit caused by vacillation between alpha and theta frequencies, the wave-forms of arousal and sleep respectively, on the verge of sleep. If it were, then the basis for these sensations might be a sort of standing wave, an interference node between two wave-fronts, a frequency confusion tantamount to a montage of two separate levels of consciousness.

Alternatively, these somatic distortions could be caused by dissipating waves of excitation diffusing outwards from the fading anthropocephalon, temporarily exciting adjacent & then faraway sections of the brain, like concentric ripples travelling outwards from a disturbance in a pond. It could be that the intense & focalized neurochemical processes of the anthropocephalon, diffusing outwards at the onset of sleep, are a part of the progressive disengagement of consciousness. Sleep, by neutralizing focal usage, would act as a method of maintaining homeostasis, a symmetrical equilibrium of excitation. The wave of heightened excitation suffusing into the rest of the brain from the anthropocephalon would be like an electrochemical evening breeze stirring the curtains in the room representing the somatosensory cortex.

'Yin/yang' states are also common at the edge of sleep, although they seem to have some deeper noetic purpose, a primal existential function. Typically yin/yang instances follow on fantasies with a strong visual component and are most marked during adolescence. As one lies in bed with one's eyes closed, one might visualize a walk in the country perhaps, or a group of people, and this inward fantasy will occasionally develop into a yin/yang sequence, that is, gradually assuming the form of an involuntary daydream. At this point the evoked visual component is strong enough to appear as eidetic imagery, like the interplay of coloured lights one sometimes sees with one's eyes closed. Yin/yang imagery consists of the fleeting succession of contrary or opposite visual textures with accompanying mood affects. The country walk would develop into a forest scene successively alternating in appearance between jagged, high-contrast textures and smooth, pale, attenuated shapes and textures. With human figures, pale, washed-out tall bodies would alternate with chunky, black-and-white short figures.

Either extreme of these mildly involuntary eidetic sequences is truly hellish in aspect. Each represents a tactile realm both alien & inhuman. In these instances hell is the inability to mediate the two extremes.

The Sensory Homunculus

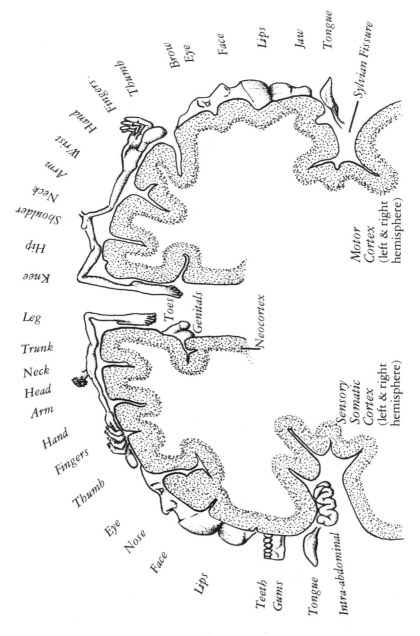

The Anthropic Canon—A Cosmology

This is the ideal world for the the idea.

The Sensory Homunculi of Animals

Rabbit

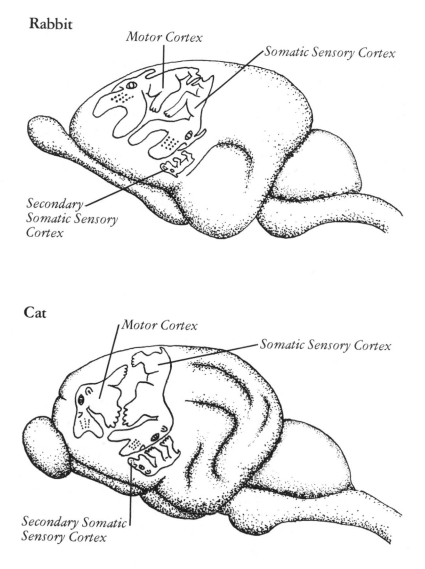

Motor Cortex

Somatic Sensory Cortex

Secondary Somatic Sensory Cortex

Cat

Motor Cortex

Somatic Sensory Cortex

Secondary Somatic Sensory Cortex

Acquisitional Vulnerability

Consciousness is vulnerable during acquisitional stages. Child-
hood is the obvious acquisitional stage though the neurohormo-
nal turmoil of adolescence is perhaps even more acute. States of
revelation, even in the fully grown adult, can be spoken of as
acquisitional states & provide a suitably unstable site for vulner-
ability to neurosis or depression. It is an inherent weakness of
the species, the prolonged childhood renders the human not
only vulnerable in the physical sense, but also vulnerable to
disorders of perception & cognition.

Hallucinations are the involuntary metaphorizations of a distressed mind.

History & the Collective Mind; a Neurohormonal Community

Human history is perhaps the record of mass reversals of polarity between inhibitory & excitatory domination of the collective mind. Vast, dipolar waves sweeping through the collective mind in storms of excitation & inhibition, like high & low pressure cells in weather systems, moving over continents & through peoples. The flow of pure history defined in the ebb & wax of these tides, the glittering neurochemical host.

Knowledge is Lamarckian.

Pets

A pet is a detachable tactile surface which can be 'disowned' as having 'a will of its own'. This frees the animal to act as an intermediary tactile surface effecting social transactions between humans.

Pets are also a form of sensory augmentation. The symbiotic sensory array of man and dog is much more effective than either creature by itself.

Municipal Hormone Loops

The grid of the city is a control structure. Overcrowding precipitates higher hormonal activity in the individual. Self-assertion in aggressive public transit environments leads to stressful levels of adrenal hormones. The constant violation of individual physical privacy, the result of competition for placement in line-ups, leads to muscle armouring and protective, ultimately bent, postures. Excitedness and adrenalin are kinds of polisbinding links, a sort of biologically enforced patriotism, locking the citizen into the high population density urban matrix.

The function of police, of all sirened vehicles in fact, is to inject adrenalin into circulation, maintain the 'high' of background fear. The professional classes maintain this same high with news, an all-news station providing a constant low key adrenalin rush, like an intravenous drip. This elevated vigilance, inherent in the dilute aggressive state of the ordinary citydweller, is similar to the action of amphetamine. Security, which unlike health care is not universal, has become an industry which entrenches paranoia & isolation.

The city is a vast corporate hormonal loop. Mass levels of gonadotropins are manipulated by erotic advertising. Elevated levels of endorphins in jogging executives anaesthetize their social conscience. Unbridled smooth muscle aggression, along with elevated military spending levels, triggered the recession of the early 80's.

The mascot of the hormonal village is the psychopath, charming, witty, guiltless & deadly.

Facial Features

As most people age, their faces permanently assume the dominant emotion of their lives, reflect their mean emotive posturing. On public transit one sees too much servile resignation. Like actors in the theatre of our lives we grow into a role, our faces a caricature of a fictional identity we affect in order to cope with reality.

What strange shapes we assume in order to survive. And out of the total spectrum of human potential for personality what strange ecological niches we seem to carve for ourselves.

Facial features themselves are signifiers, though qualified as such only by their presence or absence. Individual variation is as variable as individuality. Visages can differ wildly, monstrously & yet a face will still be recognized and treated as such. Lipstick will be applied to the edges of the cavity beneath the nose, ears will generally appear on either side of the head.

Template Matching

The domination of human perception by idealized forms can be appreciated by observing the template matching phenomenon as it is manifest in fashion. Certain physiologies typify particular eras, an ideal body becomes the somatic reflection of an external fashion. There is ample evidence for an archetypal semiology in the consensus of choice for the 'ideal solid'. The ideal template is held up in front of every person observed in daily transactions. This means that variance, when perceived, is viewed as monstrous, to be safe is to be identified with the ideal type, of which a separate form exists for all ages, social groupings and classes. This template is an extension of symbolic logic acting in areas which are not properly its domain. In human beings variation is the norm. This variation is viewed as monstrous or entropic by the viewers who implicitly subscribe to the alibi of serial ideal templates.

Mutation as Ground of the Ideal

Mutation is the medium of the *ideal*. It provides the material, the variance, from which taste is conjured. In other words, without variation there could be no comparison amongst types within species, and without comparison a relative hierarchy cannot be established. A societally held ideal template is a supramodal, symbolic system operating paradoxically within a biological context.

Fashion is the necessity of chance.

Terato-skópos

In ancient Mesopotamia there were handbooks which catalogued common mutations and the sequelae which they portended. Terato-skópos was the name for this practice of divination by prodigies or monstrous births.

Implicit in the idea of terato-skópos is the idea that variation from average appearance is an event laden with semiological content, which posits *a priori* the concept of human & animal features as having average genetic appearance and as such being a specific relation of signifiers susceptible, by mutation, to impression by invisible forces. In a sense mutations do foretell the future, though in a gradual Darwinian sense. Mutation as sign takes features as signifiers.

If mutation is the ground of the ideal, or at least the ground of evolution in the cosmic-ray-mutative-engine-of-evolution sense, then these ancients knew it covertly and verified their intuitions by exalting mutation into the apotheosis of divine will, the invisible world of teleological portent.

Difference as Information

Chance breeds the unique. The dissimilarity of the rare object poses a distance from the ordinary mind that is filled with pure difference.

As humans it is our similarity that allows communication. Difference gives us something to communicate.

The constants we discern within the infinite variation of the world become its icons. These signs are perceptual generalizations which operate as discursive tools for manipulating the reality they codify. Our ideals are idols of arrested variation in a temple of stasis, of hallucinatory permanence.

Predators

The predator has been the major evolutionary modifier of the sensory apparatus.

The human is an ironic predator of the adoration where prey is nascent in the world.

Survival of the propitious.

Religion

Every religion is an organism with its own procreative strategy for survival. The means of its reproduction can assume one of several dominant modes. It can disseminate itself through proselytization, through missionary work or through evangelism. It is essential that these reproductive modes are entrenched in a written corpus in order to survive the vagaries of oral transmission and the inherent mutation it entails.

The fecundity or strength of a religion, its potency, can be measured by how well it survives without resorting to aggressive conversion campaigns where the survival of the organism is insured merely by numbers of adherents, like certain types of vermin that lay thousands upon thousands of eggs to insure the survival of at least one or two of their progeny. In fact, one can determine the spiritual profundity of any given religion merely by examining its mode of transmission, the energy it expends to survive as a discrete entity.

The World Soul

The world soul always establishes itself in the emptiest cultural or media structure available, it flows through the medium of least resistance. The world soul moves strongly in the intellectual lacunae of creativity. It will manifest itself in the most mindless of pop songs, trapped in the hollow spaces in the radio waves, the spaces between to reach us so coldly.

Entropy & Limerance

The second law of thermodynamics states that the entropy (disorder) of a closed system increases with time. The universe can be regarded as a finite system.

Phenylethylamine is a neurochemical which has been detected in the brains of people who are in love. It is thought to be the mediator of limerance, an intense obsession with another person. It is present in minute quantities in chocolate.

Love

Love is a consensual domain. A phenylethylamine fix fluttering at the interface of entropy & negentropy. As such it is an anomaly in the second law of thermodynamics which governs biological events as surely as it governs the inanimate universe.

The proximity of love to perpetual motion is the unrelenting incentive for consummation and is called lust.

The structural coupling of two lovers is determined by the confluence of their ideals of each other. Their arousal activates a prehensile field over the entire body surface. The erotic charge is directly proportional to the ability to localize total consciousness in specific somatic sites. Consummation is the irresistible consequence of a series of bio-chemical reactions, it is the interlocking of both their bio-chemical & ontological domains.

Suspended consummation is pure energy.

Love

Love is an exquisite loneliness. It is the combination of two lonelinesses into one vast loneliness greater than the sum of its parts. Love is an exultation in the sheer existential magnitude of itself, which is as vast and empty as the night sky. This is why lovers identify themselves with celestial bodies.

Two is the loneliest number of all.

I love our you.

True Heart, Cruel Heart

Only the ultra-sane can afford reality. Only the sane, with that manic edge that depressives would insist on calling psycho-pathological, can withstand, while maintaining a position of pure faith, determinate reality. That which we call the 'self' is purely the product of neurological activity in the brain, an epiphenomenon. Consciousness is to the brain as the shadow is to the body. However, because consciousness can influence itself it transcends the deterministic barrier of pure materialism.

Consciousness can crawl back through the mirror & truly inhabit the paradox of doubled being, of self consciousness. Our consciousness, perceived as immaterial & able to engage in the most ironic of self-speculations, is at root composed of the same infinite energy & light which fuels the heart. As the brain is to thought and the genitals are to sex, so is the heart unto truth.

When we know this, our natural empathy for other human beings is increased exponentially, for we can totally identify with their existence relative to an absolute reality. We are all the products of a miraculous evolution whose engine was cosmic chance. For when you have stripped yourself down to your original self the universe will become a lattice of information, in every part consistently different from itself, where you need look for miracles no further than your own hands.

You will see everything as an occasion, all objects will become events, a rock or planet merely occupying a location & volume for a period of time. You will be able to apprehend the entire being of the men and women you meet. If you look into their eyes you will see everything they have done and who they are. And some eyes will appear like fractured glass, impervious to your gaze. And others will be sensual ports on beings you will instantly love.

Glossary

adrenalin   A hormone which stimulates the nervous system and heightens alertness.

afferent   Incoming impulses. That part of a neuron which receives incoming impulses.

alpha waves   Alpha waves characterize the electrical activity in the brain of a mature, conscious human. They are in the range of 8 to 13 cycles per second.

angular gyrus   A convolution in the left temporal lobe thought to associate the visual form of a letter with the corresponding auditory pattern.

antedation   Assigning an earlier date than the true one to a document or event. In the context of the brain it is utilized by Libet (1973) to explicate his theory regarding the brain's processing of sensory stimuli. Libet's hypothesis, based on the cortical processing of weak skin stimuli, was that although a stimulus required .5 seconds of cortical activity in order to be experienced (the minimum human reaction time) in the experiencing process it was antedated by being referred in time back to the arrival of the original signal in the brain! In this retrograde interval, a successful biological revisionism of sorts, an apparent contradiction of chronology, John C. Eccles saw partial evidence for an immaterial mind.

anthropocephalon   The third & highest level of neural organization according to Joseph Altman's hierarchical model of mentation. Synonymous with the dominant hemisphere or the left side of the cerebral cortex. See **noetic**.

archetype   Jung's term explicating the thoughts and imagery arising from the 'collective unconscious' of mankind.

arcuate fasciculus   The bundle of nerve fibres which connect *Wernicke's* and *Broca's* areas, the two main speech centres.

artificial intelligence   Referred to as 'AI' by most researchers it consists of research into the means of reproducing intelligent machines with the ultimate goal of producing an intelligent, sentient consciousness.

associational train   In thought it is synonymous with the 'stream of consciousness' or the film-of-images, the personal sequence of ideas or fantasy. When connected with language, whose operation it is intimately bound to, it is the interior monologue.

associational tracts   Nerve fibres which form the connections between the various regions of the cortex.

associative cortex   See **interpretive cortex**

Atlas moth   An Asian species and the largest of all the giant silkworm or Saturniidae moths. *Attacus,* in terms of surface area, is the largest of all insects. Its wing-span is 10 inches or more and on the tips of its forewings is the depiction of a serpent's head.

atomic particles   The smaller components of an atom, such as electrons or neutrons.

autonomic nervous system   A system of motor nerves which ennervate smooth muscle (gut, blood vessels *etc.*) and glands. It is indirectly connected to the central nervous system and is divided into the sympathetic & parasympathetic nervous systems. The skin is supplied exclusively by the sympathetic nervous system.

Broca's area   An area in the brain (anthropocephalon, frontal lobe) which, along with Wernicke's area make up the two main speech centres of the brain. The current model is that an utterance arises in Wernicke's area and is articulated in Broca's area prior to speech.

chirality   Handedness, left or right handed relativity.

cloud chamber   An apparatus filled with vapour which enables the tracks of atomic particles to be viewed directly by eye. The particles leave white vapour trails as they travel through the cloud.

communolect   The dialect of the communal mind.

consensual domain   "The domain of interlocked conducts that result from ontogenic reciprocal structural coupling between structurally plastic organisms." Humberto R. Maturana, "Biology of Language: The Epistemology of Reality", 1978.

cortex   The 'grey matter', the outermost layer of the brain. It is 2 millimetres thick and unfolds to a surface area of 1.5 square feet. The cortex embodies the highest level of integration, thought itself.

dominance   The lateral delegation of control to one hemisphere of brain. The side of the brain in which deliberation takes place, the highest executive function.

DNA   Deoxyribonucleic acid, a helix of nucleotides composed of thymine, cytosine, adenine and guanine in coded arrangements. DNA determines the structure and genetic inheritance of all living things.

efferent   Outgoing impulses, commands. That part of a neuron which transmits outgoing impulses.

ego   In this text synonymous in usage with the 'I' perceived by the self, the self-identity, psyche *etc.*

eidetic images   Retinal images which are neither *phosphenes* nor hallucinations. Mental images so intense that they are almost equivalent to observed reality.

entropy   According to the second law of thermodynamics the entropy (disorder) of a closed system increases with time.

enzyme   A complex protein which acts as a catalyst for specific chemical operations necessary to the continuation of life. In the human body there are many enzymes which orchestrate the metabolism. The complexity and intelligence of these operations seem to place these highly sophisticated & complex molecules in the realm of consciousness. They are produced within the cell and are expressed genetically by DNA.

enzyme recognition failure   The failure of an enzyme to detect a difference between molecular 'shape' of a foreign protein & one with which it enacts normal cellular transactions.

epiphenomenalism   The philosophy that consciousness is purely the product of cerebral processes and cannot alter those processes. As the shadow is to the hand so is consciousness to the brain.

fovea centralis   A section of the retina containing no rods but packed with cones on which the image at the centre of vision, the object of attention, falls. Section of acutist vision in the retina.

generative transformational grammar   A linguistic system of analysis which produces diagrams of the grammatical infrastructure of sentences by parsing the relations of subjects & predicates etc. into surface and deep components.

genetic code   The information which is encoded into DNA and which is inherited by successive generations.

guardant   A term used in heraldry to describe the position of an heraldic creature on a coat of arms. In this case it is standing on its hind legs with its body in profile facing left and the head turned to face the viewer.

haemoglobin   The respiratory protein which colours the blood scarlet. It is similar in structure to chlorophyll and cytochrome.

hippocampus   A bi-lobed structure comprising part of the limbic system in the paleocephalon region of the brain. It is essential to both the storing and retrieval of memory.

hologram   The recorded interference pattern of a split laser beam on a photographic plate which exhibits a three dimensional reproduction of the original scene when re-illuminated. If the hologram is divided into smaller pieces each will act as a window onto the unaltered, original image.

homonym   Homograph. A word which is spelled the same as another but has a different meaning, such as 'wind'.

idiotopic map   The correlative mapping of language in the speech cortex. The planar thesaurus of the individual.

insectivore   A carnivore which feeds exclusively or primarily on insects.

ionization   Ions are electrically charged atoms, atoms with either surplus or deficit of electrons. Ionization is any process which produces ions.

isomorphism   A transposition in which the information contained in one structure or system is preserved through its transformation into another. The congruence or parallels between two complex structures such that for each part of one structure there is a corresponding part of the other structure. However, the isomorphism is established by a parallel between the relation of the parts to their respective structures rather than by a parallel between the parts or the structures themselves.

kinesthesia   The sense of muscular movement which accompanies voluntary movements of the body. Here extended to include the tactile, sculptural knowledge of the world such as is exhibited by certain nocturnal animals. Owls, for example, can become habituated by familiarity with a locale and can negotiate it blind through the agency of this familiarity.

kinetic   Of motion, energy in motion.

libidinal   Of lustful desire, erotic desire.

limen   The limit beneath which any given stimulus ceases to be perceptible.

locus coeruleus   A pigmented region of cells in the upper brain stem (paleocephalon). It is associated with reward for eating and with paradoxical sleep (deep sleep). The locus coeruleus secretes noradrenalin and together with the adjacent nuclei of Raphe orchestrates the various stages of sleep. The locus coeruleus is thought to mediate inhibition of voluntary movement during dreams, its failure causes sleep-walking.

mnemonic   Aiding memory. A device or system for aiding memory.

mosaic signal   The characteristic signal/impulse relay pattern for all perception and the nervous system in general. The nervous system relies on numerous channels, each carrying a small bit of the information to be transmitted. These multiple signals are re-integrated in the cortex.

motor cortex   A strip of cortex anterior to the frontal lobes and above the temporal lobes on both sides of the brain. The motor cortex, adjacent & parallel to the somatic sensory cortex, is *efferent* and controls those parts of the body which are under voluntary control. The motor strip on one side of the brain controls the opposite side of the body. The map of the body in the motor cortex is called the motor homunculus and is distorted proportionately according to the emphasis placed by demands of precision on the respective body parts.

negentropy The opposite of entropy, the absence of entropy/disorder.

neuron A cell which is capable of originating and transmitting electrical impulses. The nervous system is composed of neurons and their connections.

neurotransmitter A chemical substance, usually an organic molecule with an indole ring, which facilitates or inhibits the propagation of impulses between neurons. The major neurotransmitters of the brain are acetycholine, dopamine, norepinephrine, serotonin and histamine.

noetic According to Joseph Altman's theory of the triune brain there are three levels of mentation. Each successive level of mentation represents a higher evolutionary modification. Thus the most primitive level, or reptilian brain, is called the *paleocephalon* and corresponds physiologically with the brain stem and limbic systems. It engages in pathic thought and is the seat of emotion, motivation and the mechanism of consciousness. The second level, or mammalian brain, is called the *neencephalon,* and corresponds physiologically with the minor or right hemisphere of the cerebral cortex. It engages in iconic thought, that is to say it deals with symbolic representations of the environment and formulates appropriate responses by matching experience with memory. Its actions can be characterized more as habitual than deliberate. The most sophisticated and evolutionarily the most recent modification is the human mind, the *anthropocephalon* or dominant hemisphere. It engages in *noetic* thought, that is to say language and high-level symbolism, human consciousness.

olfactory Of or pertaining to the sense of smell.

ontology The study of the primary characteristic of being, the essence of things. Being in the abstract.

oscilloscope   A beam of electrons electromagnetically deflected by an input (such as sound) such that the patterns reproduced on the luminescent screen of the cathode tube reflect that input.

paleocephalon   The basal level of triune mentation, the limbic system and brain stem. See **noetic.**

particle track   The trail of ionized vapour left behind by the passage of an atomic particle through a cloud chamber or cyclotron target.

phatic   A non-verbal utterance. Of emotive augmentation only.

phenylethylamine   The neurochemical thought to be the mediator of limerance, or the intense love for another human.

phosphene   The perception of a point of light by the eyes in the absence of external light sources, such as by application of pressure to the eyeballs by the fingertips.

phylogenic   The evolution of a phylum of creatures. (A phylum being the broadest classification of a group of alike animals, such as the vertebrates.)

proprioception   The perception of one's own body, specifically the kinesthetic receptors which detect position and movement.

prosthesis   An artificial limb or body part which replaces a missing or damaged limb or organ.

psilocybin   A neurotransmitter mimetic similar in structure to serotonin. An hallucinogen almost identical in its action to d-lysergic acid diethylamide.

quantum theory   The theory introduced by Max Planck that all electro-magnetic radiations are quantized, *i.e.;* composed of discrete units or quanta which behave both as particles and as waves.

recursion   Novels within novels, pictures within pictures, recently systems which loop back on themselves in a self-descriptive manner.

return stroke   Lightning. A massive flow of electrons moving in the opposite direction of the original or main leader of lightning after the leader has established a conduit.

saturniidae moths   Generally the largest & most beautiful moths in any given locale. Giant moths which are often mistaken for butterflies.

second law of thermodynamics   Heat cannot be transferred through a continuous, self-sustaining process from a cooler to a hotter body. In a closed system entropy (disorder) increases with time.

somatic   Of the body, bodily.

somatic sensory cortex   A strip of cortex anterior to the frontal lobes and above the temporal lobes on both sides of the brain. The somatic sensory cortex, adjacent and parallel to the motor cortex, is *afferent* and receives and processes signals from the body. The somatic sensory cortex on one side of the brain receives information from the opposite side of the body. The map of the body in the somatic sensory cortex is called the somatic sensory homunculus and is distorted proportionately according to the emphasis placed by the demands of precision on the respective body parts.

somatotopic homunculus   The somatic sensory and motor homunculi, the map realized on the cortextual surface by the correspondence of bodily parts to their mediatory areas in the motor & somatic sensory cortexes.

somnambulistic   Of sleep, the performing of actions or talk during sleep.

spoiler   A design affectation of North American and European cars in the late seventies and early eighties where the chassis rises into a thin inclined plane at the posterior end of the car. An 'aerodynamic' ornament similar to the fins on cars produced in the late fifties and early sixties. Thought to keep the rear wheels of the car on the ground at high speeds.

Stepping Razor   Title of a song by Jamaican reggae singer Peter Tosh. In the film *Rockers* this song was the soundtrack for the visual documentation of several Jamaican "rastas" walking. Their walk was an accentuated dance of lateral asymmetry. It seemed to me that to walk 'stepping razor' was to acknowledge lateral dominance.

striate cortex   Formerly the occipital lobe. The section of the cortex which processes visual information.

symbiosis   The exclusive fusion of two dissimilar organisms to the end of mutual benefit.

synesthesia   The apprehension of one sense as having the same characteristics as another, such as of a particular sound having an association with a certain colour.

thalamus   The uppermost section of the brainstem, part of the paleocephalon, which houses the 'junctions' of many neural pathways/tracts from the various regions of the cortex.

transubstantiation   The transformation of an object in which its substance is materially replaced by another substance, as in fossilization.

virus   A borderline unit of life possessing in many cases only half the full genetic complement of DNA necessary to reproduce itself. It must of necessity parasitize cells & use their genetic material in order to reproduce. The common cold is the manifestation of a viral infection.

Wernicke's area   An area of the cortex on the dorsal/posterior section of the temporal lobe which is one of the two primary speech centres, the other being Broca's area. It is thought to evoke the formulation of a spoken utterance, the 'draft' of an idea to be vocalized.